Ms. Donna M. Sageman
158 Westland Dr.
Bad Axe, MI 48413

Walking with Jesus

Walking with Jesus

A Member's Guide in the Community of Christ

Presented to:_____

On the occasion of:_____

_____

By:_____

Date:_____

Community of Christ

Scripture Quotations

The scripture quotations contained herein are from the New Revised Standard Version Bible, copyright © 1989 by the Division of Christian Education of the National Council of the Churches of Christ in the USA and are used by permission. All rights reserved.

Acknowledgments

Walking with Jesus is a disciple's guide for following Jesus Christ and participating in the Community of Christ. It represents the work of the following writers: Danny Belrose, Andrew Bolton, Anthony Chvala-Smith, Stassi Cramm, Jane Gardner, Robert Kyser, Bruce Lindgren, Tammy Lindle, Dale Luffman, Jerry Nieft, and David Schaal. Their contribution, along with Jerry Nieft's editorial coordination, is greatly appreciated.

ISBN 0-8309-1105-7
Copyright © 2004
Community of Christ
1001 W. Walnut
Independence, MO 64050
Printed in the United States of America
Cover Painting by Amber Mills

Contents

Foreword 11

Chapter One: Welcome! 13

Chapter Two: Becoming a Disciple of Jesus Christ 21

Chapter Three: Learning the Sacred Story 29

Chapter Four: Hearing God's Call 35

Chapter Five: Living Sacramentally 41

Chapter Six: Growing in Community 47

Chapter Seven: Participating Faithfully 55

Chapter Eight: Generosity—Sharing Our Witness 61

Chapter Nine: Generosity—Sharing Our Resources ... 69

Chapter Ten: Serving in the Mission of Christ 75

Chapter Eleven: Basic Beliefs of the Community of Christ 81

Foreword

The First Presidency is pleased to present *Walking with Jesus: A Member's Guide in the Community of Christ*. It is offered as a disciple's guide to those who have recently joined with us in our journey with Christ. We believe it will also be helpful and encouraging to those who made their decision to follow Christ some time ago. Walking with Jesus can be presented at baptism and can be used for devotional or study purposes. It is offered to everyone who seeks to follow Jesus Christ and participate with us in the Community of Christ.

The First Presidency

Chapter One:
Welcome!

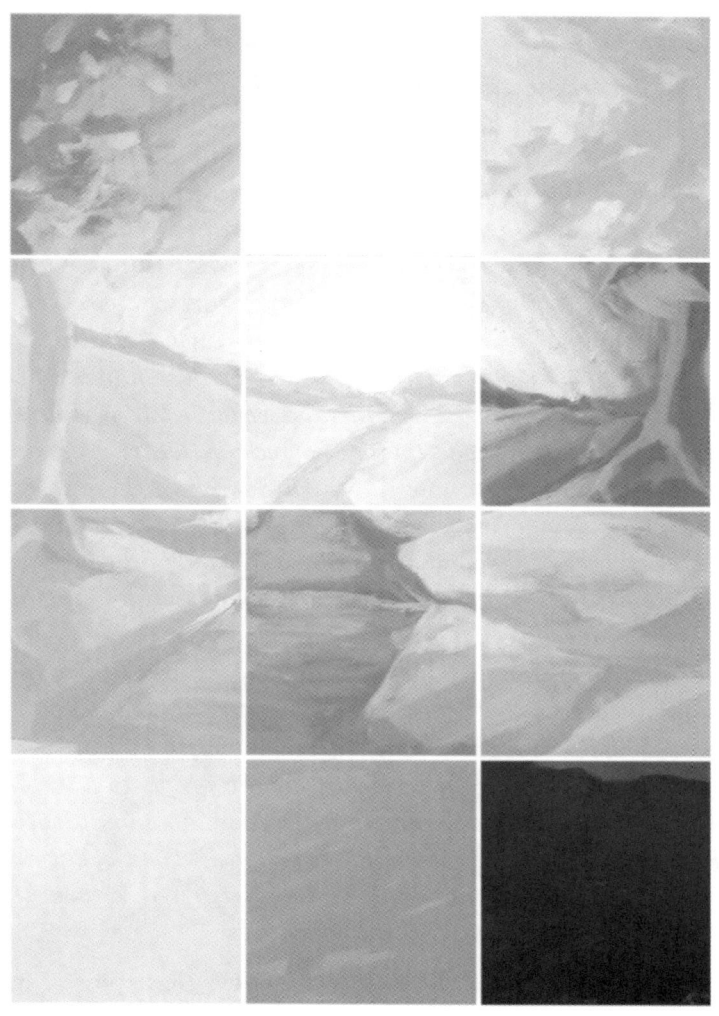

Scriptures for Reflection

Now on that same day two of them were going to a village called Emmaus, about seven miles from Jerusalem, and talking with each other about all these things that had happened. While they were talking and discussing, Jesus himself came near and went with them, but their eyes were kept from recognizing him. And he said to them, "What are you discussing with each other while you walk along?" They stood still, looking sad. Then one of them, whose name was Cleopas, answered him, "Are you the only stranger in Jerusalem who does not know the things that have taken place there in these days?" He asked them, "What things?" They replied, "The things about Jesus of Nazareth, who was a prophet mighty in deed and word before God and all the people, and how our chief priests and leaders handed him over to be condemned to death and crucified him. But we had hoped that he was the one to redeem Israel. Yes, and besides all this, it is now the third day since these things took place. Moreover, some women of our group astounded us. They were at the tomb early this morning, and when they did not find his body there, they came back and told us that they had indeed seen a vision of angels who said that he was alive. Some of those who were with us went to the tomb and found it just as the women had said; but they did not see him." Then he said to them, "Oh, how foolish you are, and how slow of heart to believe all that the prophets have declared! Was it not necessary that the Messiah should suffer these things and then enter into his glory?" Then beginning with Moses and all the prophets, he interpreted to them the things about himself in all the scriptures.

As they came near the village to which they were going, he walked ahead as if he were going on. But they urged him strongly, saying, "Stay with us, because it is almost evening

and the day is now nearly over." So he went in to stay with them. When he was at the table with them, he took bread, blessed and broke it, and gave it to them. Then their eyes were opened, and they recognized him; and he vanished from their sight. They said to each other, "Were not our hearts burning within us while he was talking to us on the road, while he was opening the scriptures to us?" That same hour they got up and returned to Jerusalem; and they found the eleven and their companions gathered together. They were saying, "The Lord has risen indeed, and he has appeared to Simon!" Then they told what had happened on the road, and how he had been made known to them in the breaking of the bread.
—Luke 24:13–35

Lift up your eyes and fix them on the place beyond the horizon to which you are sent. Journey in trust, assured that the great and marvelous work is for this time and for all time.—Doctrine and Covenants 161:1a

Welcome to the Community of Christ. We are disciples of Jesus Christ, and we invite you to walk with us as we journey with Christ through our lives. Our experience is an adventure. Our witness is the witness of the ancient church and today's church: "He lives!" Jesus Christ lives and comes with us on our journey. In the fellowship of his presence and our community, we have peace today and hope for tomorrow. We are learning to live the principles of the good news Jesus proclaimed. We are the Community of Christ.

The Journey to Emmaus

In the scripture reflection from Luke 24:13–35, two disciples have an experience with Jesus that is like ours. At some point they had become aware of Jesus' teaching and considered him to be a great teacher or prophet. They had hoped he would be the one to free Israel from its foreign rulers. However, they had been in Jerusalem recently during the dark days when Jesus was condemned, tried, and crucified. They were disappointed and depressed. They left Jerusalem for Emmaus. While walking there, they talked about what had happened and told the story to a fellow traveler. A major piece of their story was that some disciples had discovered on the third day after Jesus' death that his body was no longer in the tomb. To add to their amazement, the disciples had seen angels who said Jesus was alive.

The interested traveler entered into their discussion. He helped them understand the scriptures and how they applied to their recent experience. They had such a good experience sharing and learning that they asked him to stay with them when they arrived at Emmaus. When they sat at table to eat, the traveler blessed and broke the bread. In that moment, the disciples recognized him as Jesus. Then he vanished.

The disciples realized that the companion on their journey had been Jesus, the one for whom they were grieving. He spent time with them by giving them his personal presence. They realized that their sharing with him had warmed their hearts, just as they had been warmed on previous occasions by his presence and teaching. They suddenly knew—Jesus lived! They could not wait. They returned to Jerusalem to tell about their experience. When they arrived back, the other disciples had seen Jesus too. As they compared stories together in their little community of disciples, Jesus came to them again. And over the weeks, months, and years that followed, Jesus continued to be present with them in spirit and in fact. They came to know him to be more than they had originally expected. They acknowledged him as God's Son. They followed his example, his teaching, and his commandments. They worshiped him as Lord and Savior. They lived as his disciples, known to the world eventually as Christians.

Today we in the Community of Christ are walking on our journey to Emmaus. We have all had disappointments and loss. We study the scriptures and try to understand the events in our lives. It is our testimony that Jesus comes and reveals himself often to us as we continue our journey and open up to his Spirit. He reveals himself in our fellowship, in our study, in our breaking of bread, and in our serving others. We have encounters of recognition and a warming of the heart that motivates us to share our experiences with others. Together we celebrate the good news that Jesus proclaimed: that the kingdom of God is here and now. It is here and now when we receive Jesus Christ and become his disciples. It is here and now that we can begin to enjoy the blessings of the kingdom of God on earth.

Becoming Like Christ

As disciples of Jesus Christ, we choose to become more like Christ, and we choose to live our lives together in community—the church. Disciples are people who follow, learn from, and imitate their teacher. We know Jesus to be more than a teacher, more than a prophet, and more than a good man. We believe him to be all of what we can know of God while we are yet in this life. Therefore, Jesus' teachings are more than theory or good thoughts to us. We value them as life-giving disciplines or patterns of living for us. When we have experiences with Christ and each other, we become close in spirit and purpose. Through our living experience of being disciples, we develop core values that become part of the culture of our church community.

Our Community Values

The Community of Christ shares a common heritage with other Christian churches and also cherishes many unique values that have come from its own history of responding to its calling. Throughout its journey, the Community of Christ has learned to value and affirm certain core understandings that give it special place and purpose. These affirm what is ultimately meaningful to us—who we are and what we are about.

- Jesus Christ is central to us. Jesus' life, ministry, and teachings; his death, resurrection, and living presence are the foundation of our church. It is he who calls us, commissions us, and gives us the ability to be his disciples.
- We are connected in a wonderful fellowship. Our common experience of the Holy Spirit in our community allows us to feel a special connection and kinship to one another. We belong to one another, and we are at home with one another, no matter where we might be in the world.
- We experience the prophetic Spirit. God's Spirit continues to call, challenge, direct, and transform us today, just as in times past.
- We proclaim the worth of each person. Jesus Christ died for all and lives for all. Everyone is welcome, no exceptions. God loves us, and we love each other. Our love is lived out by respecting all people and seeking their well being.
- All disciples are needed to bring ministry. We affirm that each person has unique gifts and ministries to offer in the Community of Christ. The Holy Spirit calls and empowers each one of us as a person of worth. Each of us is wanted and needed for ministry only we can offer.
- We commit our whole life to Jesus Christ and the cause of the kingdom of God on earth. Everything that we are and do relates ultimately to our promise to follow Jesus. How we treat the world, other people, and ourselves reflects our relationship with him.
- We believe it is crucial for us to be disciples who act like disciples. Our Christian living and witness matter. God works with us in our individual and community ministries to transform the world into God's kingdom on earth.
- God continues to do new things with us. Therefore we expect that we will learn new things, be called to new ministries, and be surprised by the fresh newness that comes from a disciple's living and growing relationship with God.

As you continue to explore what it means to be and live as a disciple of Jesus Christ, be assured that Jesus travels with you to the future horizons of your life experience. Lift up your eyes and enter the path that leads to God's kingdom. Welcome to the Community of Christ.

Chapter Two: Becoming a Disciple of Jesus Christ

Scriptures for Reflection

As many of you as were baptized into Christ have clothed yourselves with Christ. There is no longer Jew or Greek, there is no longer slave or free, there is no longer male and female; for all of you are one in Christ Jesus.—Galatians 3:27–28

For the gate by which you should enter is repentance and baptism by water; and then comes a remission of your sins by fire and by the Holy Ghost. Then are you in this strait and narrow path which leads to eternal life; you have entered in by the gate; you have done according to the commandments of the Father and the Son; and you have received the Holy Ghost which witnesses of the Father and the Son, to the fulfilling of the promise which he has made that if you entered in by the way, you shall receive. Now, my beloved brethren, after you have gotten into this strait and narrow path, I would ask if all is done? Behold, I say to you, No; for you have not come thus far save it were by the word of Christ, with unshaken faith in him, relying wholly upon the merits of him who is mighty to save. Wherefore, you must press forward with a steadfastness in Christ, having a perfect brightness of hope, and a love of God and of all men.—II Nephi 13:24–29

Baptism and Confirmation— The Formal Start of Discipleship

Becoming a disciple of Jesus means accepting God's incredible love for you and learning to trust and depend on God. The decision to commit your life to follow Jesus Christ through baptism is a fundamental first step. Being a brand-new disciple of Jesus is a little like finding your place on a map with the designation "you are here" highlighted at a small spot and realizing that you are surrounded by what seems like a world of endless possibilities. In reality, Christian discipleship does have boundaries, but it is also full of choices and amazing opportunities. Each day we make choices that affect how we live and express our discipleship. As we find our way along the path of opportunities that are ahead, it is important to learn, worship, pray, develop relationships with other disciples, and understand that Christ is always with us.

Disciples of Jesus Christ are baptized and confirmed as a way to follow Christ's example.

> Jesus began his work by asking to be baptized (Matthew 3:12–17). A person seeking to be baptized recognizes God's personal love and forgiveness through Jesus Christ. A lifelong covenant or promise is made to follow Christ. We are immersed in water to symbolize death to sin and raised out of the water to begin a new life. Paul, an early convert to Christianity, wrote how baptism symbolizes a complete following of Jesus and a dramatic change of life; "…when you were buried with him in baptism, you were also raised with him through faith in the power of God…" (Colossians 2:12).
> —*Seekers and Disciples*, Independence, Missouri: Herald House, 2001, 36

> Jesus promises to those who would follow as disciples, the Holy Spirit, "another Advocate, to be with you forever. This is the Spirit of truth…" (John 14:16–17). After baptism by water, elders of the congregation place their hands on the head of the disciple and offer a special prayer. Through this confirming the disciple receives the guidance and blessing of God's Spirit for strength to keep the baptismal covenant.…—*Seekers and Disciples*, 37

Baptism and confirmation are often regarded as highlights in a person's life. While these two significant events mark the formal start of the disciple's journey, it is good to remember they are just that—a place to start. What follows baptism and confirmation is of great importance. It is here that the journey really begins. It is here that we each take our next steps as disciples.

Covenant—Living Out the Meaning of Baptism

The commitment we make at baptism is part of a two-part agreement or promise, sometimes called a covenant. God promises us that the Holy Spirit will always be present with us to help us in our discipleship. We agree to be followers of Jesus, and we try to live each day as his disciple.

Following the example and teachings of Jesus will change our lives. We will think about things in new ways, see and care for the world differently, share with an expanding circle of friends, make better decisions about how to live our lives, and encounter amazing opportunities. However, discipleship will not make us perfect or guarantee that life will be free of pain or tough choices. Disciples experience many of the same challenges of everyday living as they did before baptism. In this way we are still connected with those who are not yet baptized. We live in the same world and encounter similar issues and choices; it is part of being human. During trying times we discover we are connected to a Christian family of believers. We are all part of God's family. We can rely on both the support of a faith community and the presence of the Holy Spirit to help guide our actions and decisions.

How we live makes a difference to us and to those around us. Knowing God is with us will affect the choices we make. We can expect our lives will change when we become disciples. We view issues of education, health, finances, friends, family, career, politics, and other life choices through new eyes. We ask, "How will having Christ in my life affect how I react to situations I encounter?" and "If God is with me, what can I do now that I couldn't do before?" In essence we are no longer living just for ourselves; we are living in Christ and for others.

Communion—The Disciple's Renewal

The journey of discipleship is not without struggles. As with any other discipline, Christian disciples sometimes stumble. We often slip and miss the mark of following Christ's teachings. We may feel disconnected or separated from God when times get hard or when choices we make present problems. It is a bit like losing our place on the map; we need to take steps to find our way again. Ironically, it is during these times that Christians find significant opportunity to reconnect with Christ and with one another. We can count on the promise of God's Spirit to always be with us. We can choose to fix the things that are wrong. We can say we are sorry for mistakes or misunderstandings. We can celebrate again the commitment we made in baptism by experiencing Communion, or the Lord's Supper—one of Christ's greatest gifts. It is a gift of memory repeatedly made fresh and alive, offered to us by Jesus in his last meal with his disciples:

> Then he took a loaf of bread, and when he had given thanks, he broke it and gave it to them, saying, "This is my body, which is given for you. Do this in remembrance of me." And he did the same with the cup after supper, saying, "This cup that is poured out for you is the new covenant in my blood."—Luke 22:19–20

Through the Communion experience, Christian believers are linked. It is the act of being God's people, together. It is in the Communion experience that we partake of the bread and wine—symbols of Jesus' body and his sacrifice for us. It is during Communion that we can reclaim the promise we made at baptism and remember Jesus, his sacrifice, and his promise to us. Communion is a chance to become clean again, to "come back" to Christ, or to start over. It is in moving beyond mistakes or times of trial that we learn and grow, find our place again, and then move forward in our service to Christ and others.

Expectations— Connecting the Disciple with Life Issues

Many people in today's culture associate the idea of membership with what they know about membership in various organizations. They think of paying dues, following rules, and acting in ways that are no longer meaningful. On the contrary, the apostle Paul viewed members of the church metaphorically as vital organs in a whole, living body. Members or disciples belong to an organic living body rather than an institution. We belong in living relationship with God, Jesus, and each other.*

Being a disciple of Jesus Christ comes first. Out of our relationship with him comes the desire to do something meaningful. Disciples are not passive. Discipleship by its very definition involves purposeful action. When we agreed to follow Jesus Christ, we were in essence agreeing to be disciples who act for their Lord. As members of Christ's church—the living body of Christ in the world—we need to understand that we are not alone in God's work. We each play a vital part in living out Jesus' examples and teaching. At the heart of the disciple's mission are the following goals:

- Share your witness. Invite others to church activities; share what being a disciple means to you.

- Share your resources. Prioritize and wisely manage your spending so you can save and give generously.

- Worship. Regularly share together in congregational worship; engage in personal devotion, scripture study, and prayer.

- Be involved. By working and sharing together in congregations and communities, we experience a deeper understanding of who God calls us to be.

- Learn and teach. Continually seek to understand the teachings of Jesus; share in educational experiences; share your insights with others along the way.

- Be a peacemaker. Seek peace within yourself; learn skills to bring peace to situations where conflict threatens relationships; promote peace and seek justice.

—Adapted from "Being a Disciple,"
Community of Christ tract (2003)

Stages of Discipleship

As members of Christ's family, we should be aware that progress and understanding come at different stages. Each disciple's journey is unique. We each develop and grow differently, and are at different stages of seeking, finding, and discipling. We can never fully know everything. As we grow, learn, and test new understandings, we must remember to be patient with ourselves, with other disciples, and with those who are not yet disciples. A belief that we cling to today may be reconsidered tomorrow, next month, or next year in the light of our new experience. Change is part of growing. It is a little like becoming familiar with the map and "where we are." Over time, with experience, finding our way becomes easier and our destination more clear.

As you progress, allow yourself room to grow. Try, and do not be afraid to make mistakes. Salvation is not based on getting everything right or making no mistakes: it is the gift of God offered to us in grace and mercy. Remember, your need for God looks and feels different at various stages of your life. Ask for help and give help to those who ask. Remember that discipleship is a process. Trust that God is working with you and with others.

---

*Rick Warren, *The Purpose-Driven Church: Growth without Compromising Your Message and Mission,* (Grand Rapids, Michigan: Zondervan, 1995), 310.

Chapter Three:
Learning the Sacred Story

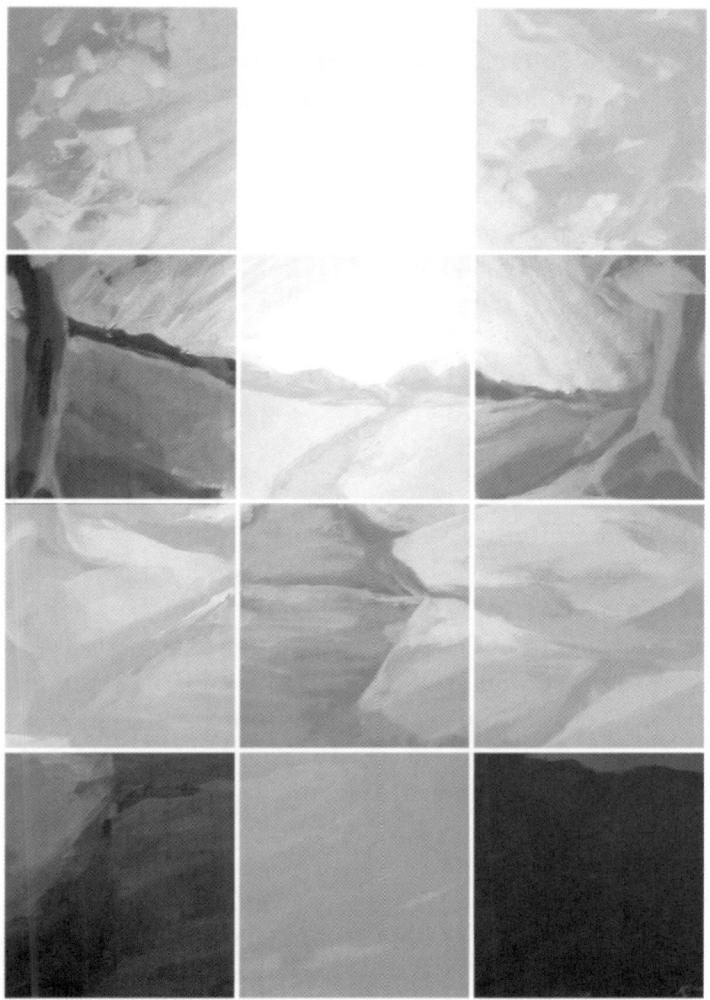

Scriptures for Reflection

All scripture is inspired by God and is useful for teaching, for reproof, for correction, and for training in righteousness, so that everyone who belongs to God may be proficient, equipped for every good work.—II Timothy 3:16–17 NRSV

Test my words. Trust in my promises for they have been given for your assurance and will bear you up in times of doubt.
—Doctrine and Covenants 155:7

To follow Jesus faithfully we need training, correction, and assurance. We need to steep our minds and imaginations in Jesus' life and ministry. We need to remind ourselves often of the high calling that is ours as his disciples. And we especially need encouraging words for those times when we stumble and make mistakes. For centuries Christians have found all this and more by reading the scriptures.

What Is Scripture?

The word "scripture" literally means "things written." The scriptures are a collection of writings that Christians recognize as having special value for guiding them in their faith. The scriptures come to us from human authors. The early Christian church preserved and selected the writings that would become scripture. Christians also see the scriptures as a gift that God has provided the church. Scripture tells the marvelous story of God's great love for the world. In the Community of Christ we sometimes call this story the "Sacred Story." Sacred is another word for "set apart" or "holy." The story the scriptures tell is sacred because through it we come to know God and God's purposes for the world. It is also sacred because it is inspired. To call scripture "inspired" means that God's Spirit influenced the process that brings these writings to us.

The Sacred Story comes to us in the Bible. The word "Bible"

is from a Greek word that means "the books." This term is an important reminder that the Bible is not just one book. It is a whole library of books written by many authors over many centuries. Christians divide the books of the Bible into two groups: the books of the Old Testament and those of the New Testament. A "testament" is a covenant, a special promise between two parties. The Old Testament tells how God called the people of Israel to be a light to all the nations. This task proved hard, but God was faithful to them. Israel's response to this calling prepared the way for the coming of Christ. The New Testament tells of this event. Christians believe it is the most important event of all history. Jesus of Nazareth came not only to point to God's love, but also to be God's love in person. The life, death, and resurrection of Christ reveal for all time that "God so loved the world" (John 3:16).

With other Christians, the Community of Christ uses the Bible as its foundational book. Without the witness of the Bible, we would be in the dark about who God is and what God wants for our lives. The Community of Christ is unique in that we also use two other books in addition to the Bible. These books are the Book of Mormon and the Doctrine and Covenants. We use them as scripture because we hear in their words an additional testimony of God's love for the whole world. These books confirm all that the Bible says. We have found them "useful for teaching, for reproof, for correction, and for training in righteousness." Using the Book of Mormon and Doctrine and Covenants as scripture also reminds us of an important truth: God's revelation did not stop centuries ago, when the last book of the Bible was written. The Sacred Story is still being written today because God is still revealing God's love and mercy.

Why Study Scripture?

Christians study the scriptures for at least four reasons. First, the scriptures remind us of who God is and what God calls disciples to be and become. Memory is very important to Christians.

The original events of the Sacred Story took place centuries ago. We would know little about the life and ministry of Christ apart from the witness of the Bible. While it is true that God continues to reveal love and mercy to the world, it is also true that the church's message is still the testimony of the first apostles. To be true to that message, we need to keep our memories fresh. We study scripture in order to stay faithful to the good news of Jesus Christ. Without scripture it would be easy to forget what we are called to be and do.

Second, we study the scriptures to *renew* our faith. Just as we need to eat regularly to keep our bodies strong, so reading scripture regularly keeps our faith healthy. For centuries Christians have found that prayerful, thoughtful meditation on the Sacred Story leads them again and again into the presence of God. In other words, by reading scripture we open ourselves to God's love and influence, which refreshes us on our journey. Studying scripture is like putting another log on a campfire: it keeps the fire of our faith from dying down and going out.

Third, the words of scripture *reassure* us of God's unfailing presence. The journey of discipleship is often hard. We will sometimes take wrong turns and make bad choices. Like everyone else, we will experience pain and sorrow. Sometimes it will seem to us that God is far away, and maybe even absent from our struggles. Scripture, however, teaches us that all who have responded to God's call have had to face such times. The stories of how faithful disciples from the past found courage in their darkest moments can give us strength. God's promise to be always near us will bear us up in times of doubt. Because the words of scripture have stood the test of time, they can help us stand firm in moments when all seems uncertain.

Fourth, we study the scriptures so that God's Spirit can *remake* us. Baptism does not instantly turn us into the person God has created us to be. Becoming a new creature in Christ is a life-long process. In the Gospels of Matthew, Mark, Luke, and

John, Jesus' first disciples did not know everything they needed to know the instant they said yes to following Jesus. Only by staying with him did they slowly open themselves to his influence. The testimony of generations of Christians is that studying scripture is one of the best ways we can stay close to our Lord. As we do so, the Holy Spirit will help us grow little by little into the fullness of Christ. As we daily place the Sacred Story before our minds and hearts, we become open to God's power to transform us for the sake of others.

Bible Versions

Members of the Community of Christ should use the most up-to-date translations of the Bible available. Versions such as the New Revised Standard Version and the New International Version provide students of the Bible with accurate translations based on the best current knowledge of the ancient languages in which the Bible was written. Many church members also like to use a version of the Bible that Joseph Smith felt inspired to produce, usually called the "Inspired Version." Though not a translation, this version passes on some of Joseph's insights into the meaning of certain passages in the Bible. The Inspired Version is thus an important part of the Community of Christ's heritage.

How Shall We Study Scripture?

There is much to learn in order to study and use scripture well. The Bible, for example, was written in times and places distant from our own. Grasping what the authors were trying to say will often mean that we will need to learn new skills. We will need the wisdom and experience of the Christian community to help us understand scripture in ways that benefit our discipleship. As you enter into the great voyage of learning the Sacred Story, there are two rules worth remembering. First, remember that the main *point* of scripture is to point to Jesus Christ as God's life-giving revelation to the world. We study the scriptures for no other reason than to serve him better. Second, remember that we must never worship either the scriptures or our interpretations of them. God alone is worthy of our worship. And so the most important virtue we can nurture as we read and use scripture is humility. Humility opens us as nothing else can to the treasures of the Sacred Story.

Chapter Four:
Hearing God's Call

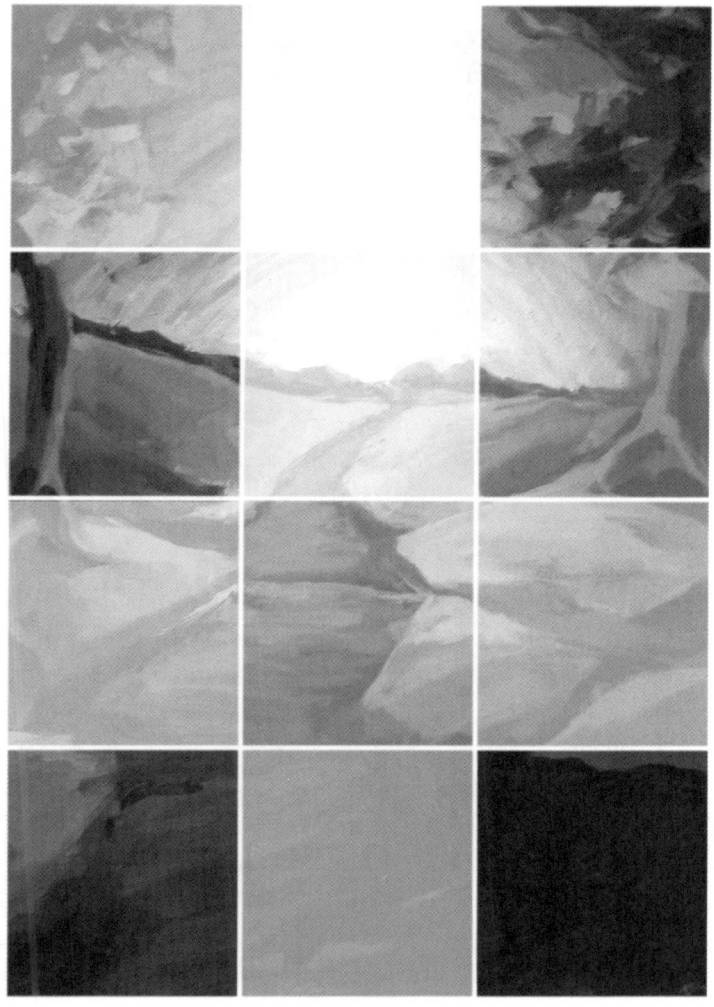

Scriptures for Reflection

As he walked by the Sea of Galilee, he saw two brothers, Simon, who is called Peter, and Andrew his brother, casting a net into the sea—for they were fishermen. And he said to them, "Follow me, and I will make you fish for people." Immediately they left their nets and followed him. As he went from there, he saw two other brothers, James son of Zebedee and his brother John, in the boat with their father Zebedee, mending their nets, and he called them. Immediately they left the boat and their father, and followed him.

—Matthew 4:18–22

All are called according to the gifts of God unto them; and to the intent that all may labor together, let him that laboreth in the ministry and him that toileth in the affairs of the men of business and of work labor together with God for the accomplishment of the work intrusted to all.

—Doctrine and Covenants 119:8b

Discipleship begins in hearing God's call and saying, "Yes!" The decision to follow Jesus informs all other decisions. It is the big "Yes!" In a sense, when we choose to travel the path of the disciple, the rest is just taking directions. In other words, we commit ourselves to this journey trusting that the Holy Spirit will open doors of transformation, opportunity, and service. Peter, Andrew, James, and John heard God's call and responded "immediately." They left their nets, their boats, and their livelihood to step out into the unknown. They would never be the same. They were to discover that God's call is an ever-present beckoning of the divine will that constantly seeks response. It was a ceaseless call that stretched them to new heights, presented them with new challenges, and surprised them with talents and abilities beyond their imagination.

"All are called according to the gifts of God unto them"

What was true for these humble fishermen is true for all who say yes to Jesus. God's call dramatically realigns life's priorities and puts us on a path to discern God's hope for creation and who God would have us be. Followers of Jesus soon realize that God's call is not frozen in time by the sweep of a pen circling the date of their baptism on a kitchen calendar. The call to be God's person is ever constant. It may come without fanfare and in many disguises—nature, art, music, poetry, a blaze of color, a touch, or a feeling—reminding us of God's investment in life and our place in it. It may be experienced in the singing of a hymn, a verse of scripture, the beauty of a sunset, the clasp of a hand, or the hope in a child's face. God's call comes as the pulse of each new day presenting us with opportunities to witness and share our resources. It comes as a challenge to explore our giftedness and to enter uncharted paths of service, such as

- teaching a church school class,
- serving on a missionary team,
- participating in a visiting program,
- planning and participating in a worship service,
- helping in the nursery,
- assisting with church budgets and finances,
- taking a leadership role, or
- volunteering for community projects.

In these avenues of stewardship (and many more), God beckons us to personal growth and development. We hear God's call to sharpen our skills, expand our knowledge, and give of our best. We read in scripture, "Seek learning even by study, and also by faith" (Doctrine and Covenants 85:36a). Participation in workshops, retreats, Temple School courses, and seminary classes helps equip us for effective service and ministry.

Hearing God's Call to Priesthood

While all members of the Community of Christ are called to ministries of service, some are called and ordained to specific priesthood responsibilities. The church's priesthood is composed of the Aaronic order, which contains the offices of deacon, teacher, and priest, and the Melchisedec order, which contains the offices of president, apostle, bishop, evangelist, high priest, seventy, and elder. Each priesthood office has a specialized function in keeping with the unique gifts and competencies of those called to serve.

Administrative officers (pastors, mission center presidents, World Church officers) initiate calls to priesthood through the spirit of inspiration and wisdom. Once calls to the priesthood have received administrative approval, candidates for ordination are informed of the call. On acceptance of the call, legislative approval by the necessary jurisdiction is sought prior to ordination. At this point candidates complete several courses of study from Temple School related to their prospective ordination. Personal discernment of one's call to priesthood may or may not precede formal processing of a call. While some individuals sense the prompting of God's Spirit that such a call is imminent, others respond affirmatively with a desire to serve, and experience God's confirming Spirit in their ministerial tasks.

Hearing a Familiar Voice

Each person is an unrepeated miracle of God's creation. God calls people in different ways. Where one may hear God clearly speaking through scripture, another may hear God's call in quiet meditation, and still another while in conversation with a child. To paraphrase what Leslie D. Weatherhead has said, "We ought to train ourselves to perceive God's comings into our deeper life, the communion of God's unseen with our unseen, by watching our thoughts, feeling, and will." He shares the following in *The Transforming Friendship:*

If I have a thought, as I go about your work, which is high, and lofty and liberating, with no meanness in it, I ought to say to myself, "[God's call] has touched my thoughts today." If I find my feelings widening so that bitterness is purged away, and I am possessed of a larger sympathy, a broad tolerance, a deep affection for all persons, then I ought to teach myself to say, "[God's call] has been near my feelings today." If I find myself no longer shrinking from an unwelcome task, telling myself that in God I am adequate for anything that may make a demand upon me, then I may say to myself, "The very fact that 'I cannot' has become 'I can,' and 'I can' has become 'I will' means, [God's call] has spoken to my will today."*

However God's call is heard, it is recognized by its familiarity. We never mistake the familiar voice of a loved one with whom we have experienced years of intimate sharing. Disciples who spend disciplined time in prayer become familiar with God's voice. We hear God clearly calling us to community, to reconciliation, to justice, to joy, hope, love, and peace.

---

*Leslie D. Weatherhead, *The Transforming Friendship* (London: Epworth Press, 1976), 55. The term "God's call" is substituted for Weatherhead's "The Friend."

Chapter Five:
Living Sacramentally

Scriptures for Reflection

Put away from you all bitterness and wrath and anger and wrangling and slander, together with all malice, and be kind to one another, tenderhearted, forgiving one another, as God in Christ has forgiven you. Therefore be imitators of God, as beloved children, and live in love, as Christ loved us and gave himself up for us....—Ephesians 4:31—5:2

Charity is the pure love of Christ, and it endures forever.... Wherefore, my beloved brothers and sisters, pray to the Father with all the energy of heart, that you may be filled with this love which he has bestowed upon all who are true followers of his Son Jesus Christ....—Moroni 7:52–53, adapted

The purpose of our Christian journey is to let the image of Christ grow in us ever more fully. God calls us to become living emblems of the love of Christ. This does not happen in a day or in a single experience. It is a lifelong process. In the past Christians have sometimes called this process "sanctification." As our salvation is the gift of God's grace, so also is our sanctification. It is the work of the Holy Spirit within us. We, however, have a role in this process too. Our role is to open ourselves in faith again and again to the love of God. To help us do this, God has placed the sacraments in the church.

What Is a Sacrament?

The sacraments are sacred rites the church celebrates. A "rite" is a special action that has spiritual meaning. The Community of Christ recognizes eight sacraments: baptism, confirmation, the Lord's Supper or Communion, laying on of hands (administration) for the sick, marriage, the blessing of children, ordination to priesthood, and the evangelist's blessing. In different ways these rites make God's love and mercy visible and available to us.

For this reason Christians sometimes call these rites a means of grace. The phrase "means of grace" is a way of saying that God's Spirit is present in these rites to help Christ's love grow in us.

What gives these rites their special, sacred character? The answer is that each of the sacraments the church celebrates traces itself to events in Jesus' ministry. Jesus was baptized by water and sent the disciples out to baptize (Matthew 3:13–17; 28: 18–20). He bestowed the Holy Spirit on his followers (20:22). On the night before his death Jesus shared a meal of bread and wine with his disciples (Mark 14:22–25). Jesus healed the sick and also sent his disciples out to anoint the sick with oil (Mark 6:13). He blessed marriage by his presence at a wedding (John 2:1–11) and by teaching that the bond between husband and wife is sacred (Mark 10:2–12). He held children in his arms and blessed them (Luke 18:15–17). Jesus chose individuals to be special representatives of his ministry (Luke 6:12–16; 10:1). And he offered a special prayer for his disciples to help and guide them in their journey (John 17; Luke 22:31–32).

The power of the sacraments comes from the one to whom they all point: Jesus Christ. These sacred rites declare the good news of the gospel. They make visible God's care and forgiveness. They give us a glimpse into ways we can understand who God is and what God calls us to be. Through them God is calling us to lives that overflow with the pure love of Christ.

Exploring the Sacraments of the Church

A closer look at each of the sacraments is now in order. Additional information is available in *Seekers and Disciples, Understanding the Way, and Doctrine and Covenants,* Section 17.

- ### Baptism

    The Community of Christ practices "believer baptism." We baptize only those who have expressed a desire to covenant with Christ to follow him all their lives. This means that baptism is for those who are old enough to make a decision to be a disciple (eight years and older). According to our understanding of baptism, priests and elders perform this rite. The proper form of baptism is complete immersion in water "in the name of the Father, and of the Son, and of the Holy Ghost."

- Confirmation

    The Community of Christ teaches that baptism is a two-part process. Baptism of the Holy Spirit follows baptism by water. Like many other Christians, we call this second rite confirmation. Following the pattern set by the apostles (see Acts 8:17), elders of the church lay their hands on the head of the new disciple and pray for the Holy Spirit's blessing. This rite "confirms" the new disciple as a full member of the Community of Christ.

- The Lord's Supper or Communion

    The Community of Christ celebrates the Lord's Supper, often called "Communion," on the first Sunday of every month. In the Lord's Supper bread and grape juice are used as emblems of Jesus' body and blood. As we recall his suffering and death, we recommit ourselves to following him. The Community of Christ practices open Communion. This means that we welcome all who believe in Christ to share in the Lord's Supper with us.

- Marriage

    The sacrament of marriage celebrates the decision of a man and a woman to be each other's companion for life. In the Community of Christ, marriage is much more than a legal arrangement. The couple pledge to live in mutual love that seeks to make real the love and compassion of Christ. Priests or elders perform this sacrament. It is available to all regardless of membership. (See Doctrine and Covenants 111.)

- Blessing of Children

    Following the example of Jesus, parents bring their little children to the elders of the church for a prayer of blessing. In this rite the elders lay their hands upon the child and ask for God's presence and guidance for both the child and parents. This sacrament typically occurs in a regular worship service and is available to all regardless of membership.

- Ordination

    Ordination confers priesthood office and authority on women and men who have been properly called and prepared. Every disciple is called to be a minister, but this sacrament sets apart some to special tasks within the church: to ministries in home and congregational life (deacons, teachers, priests); to presiding and proclaiming the gospel (elders, seventy, and high priests); to overseeing the life and witness of the larger church (bishops, apostles, and presidents); and to bringing blessing and revival (evangelists).

- Administration or Laying on of Hands for the Sick

    This sacrament opens the door to the gift of healing. Any who are sick or facing spiritual difficulties may ask elders for this special prayer. Elders anoint the head of the person with olive oil (see James 5:13–15) and pray for God's grace and blessing.

- Evangelist's Blessing

    This sacrament is unique to the Community of Christ. An individual seeking this ministry meets with an evangelist to begin preparing for this experience. When the time comes for the blessing, the evangelist lays hands on the head of the individual and offers a special prayer seeking guidance and direction for his or her life. Often this prayer is recorded and transcribed so that the individual may have a copy. Evangelist's blessings may be sought at crucial moments in one's life.

Living Sacramentally

The sacraments remind us of what it means to be a disciple of Jesus Christ. Discipleship is not about being perfect. It is first about being God's beloved children. Then as God's children, we accept the challenge of growing in the love of Christ. Following Jesus calls us to recognize our constant need for grace. It is about yielding our lives to God's purpose day by day. It is about loving God with our whole being and loving our neighbor as ourselves. What is the point of our Christian journey? It is simply this: God not only meets us in the sacraments, but God also wants to help our lives become a sacrament to the world—living emblems of the pure love of Christ. This is our high calling and great hope as disciples of Jesus Christ.

Chapter Six:
Growing in Community

Scriptures for Reflection

So Jesus called them and said to them, "You know that among the Gentiles those whom they recognize as their rulers lord it over them, and their great ones are tyrants over them. But it is not so among you; but whoever wishes to become great among you must be your servant, and whoever wishes to be first among you must be slave of all. For the Son of Man came not to be served but to serve, and to give his life a ransom for many.—Mark 10: 42–45

And it came to pass that there was no contention in the land because of the love of God which dwelt in the hearts of the people. And there were no envyings, nor strifes, nor tumults, nor whoredoms, nor lyings, nor murders, nor any manner of lasciviousness; And surely there could not be a happier people among all the people who had been created by the hand of God. There were no robbers, nor murderers, neither were there Lamanites, nor any manner of "ites"; but they were in one, the children of Christ, and heirs to the kingdom of God.
—IV Nephi 1:17–20

The path of the disciple is certainly personal, but it is far from private. Being a disciple calls us into community with one another. This community allows us to give and receive support and blend our gifts together to create a fellowship that can be a blessing to the larger community in which we live. As the scripture from Mark indicates, our church fellowship is to be characterized by mutual respect and meaningful service. To grow in this faith community, it is important that we give attention to the following things.

Ministries in Our Congregation

One of the wonderful things about the Community of Christ is that each congregation is unique according to the gifts and personalities of its members. This means that the ministries of each congregation will be unique as well. As disciples, it is important for us to be aware of the various ministries our congregation offers. Not only will we want to take advantage of these to help us in our own growth, but we may also find that our own gifts and efforts are needed to help make these ministries available to others. We need to speak with our pastor from time to time to chat about our personal interests, sense of calling, and how we might be able to help in congregational life. Sometimes this means we will help give ministry through an activity or program that already exists in the congregation. Sometimes this means we may spearhead a new effort to which we feel called to give attention, if that effort is aligned with the congregation's mission. Whatever the case may be, our pastors will appreciate the opportunity to speak with us about what the congregation is doing and how we can participate.

Worship

At the heart of growing in community is worshiping God together. In the broadest sense, worship involves the recognition and celebration that all of life is an encounter with God. The word "worship" means to "ascribe worth to," and in worship we place God at the center of our lives. A true encounter with God is more than feeling good or a therapy session. It is the beginning of a transformation from the inside out. In worship, as we focus on God, our hearts are changed and we become more aware of the need to rearrange our priorities and live different lives.

Worship services often follow the ancient, four-part model of worship found in Isaiah 6:1–8:

> In the year that King Uzziah died, I saw the Lord sitting on a throne, high and lofty; and the hem of his robe filled the temple. Seraphs were in attendance above him; each had six wings: with two they covered their faces, and with two they covered their feet, and with two they flew. And one called to another and said: "Holy,

holy, holy is the Lord of hosts; the whole earth is full of his glory." The pivots on the thresholds shook at the voices of those who called, and the house filled with smoke. And I said: "Woe is me! I am lost, for I am a man of unclean lips, and I live among a people of unclean lips; yet my eyes have seen the King, the Lord of hosts!" Then one of the seraphs flew to me, holding a live coal that had been taken from the altar with a pair of tongs. The seraph touched my mouth with it and said: "Now that this has touched your lips, your guilt has departed and your sin is blotted out." Then I heard the voice of the Lord saying, "Whom shall I send, and who will go for us?" And I said, "Here am I; send me!"

- Praise — We acknowledge God and come into God's presence with praise.
- Confession/Repentance — We confess our unworthiness and ask for forgiveness.
- Proclamation — We receive God's forgiveness and hear the word of God.
- Commitment — We give ourselves to God and commit to serving others.

As we approach a worship experience, what can we do to prepare to be active participants? A few suggestions follow.

- **Pray.** Take time individually or as a family to prepare through prayer. Pray for the needs of the congregation and ask the Holy Spirit to grace the gathering. Pray for the worship planners and those who will provide public ministry during the service. Talk to God about the concerns of your heart and the things that are keeping you from fully participating in worship.

- **Study.** Many congregations provide a listing of the six scriptures to be considered in the weekly worship service. To prepare, read through them. Particularly focus on the theme scripture. Consult a scripture commentary or other resource to learn more about the suggested scriptures. Use a children's Bible story resource or modern language version of the Bible to share Old Testament or Gospel stories as a family or with friends. Discuss what you have read.

- **Meditate.** Purposefully set aside some private time to center your thoughts and shut out distractions. Imagine being in God's presence. What does it feel like? Joy? Guilt? Fear? Peace? How do you approach the Divine? Be open and receptive, and listen for God. In conjunction with your scripture study, what insights and awarenesses come? What changes are you contemplating?

- **Participate.**
  - Come to worship expectant and enthusiastic. Expect to interact with God and the worshiping community.
  - Be present and on time. Your very presence is a ministry to others.
  - Sing the songs, recite the words, participate with the worshiping community.
  - During the service, sit with someone who is alone or visiting. Be a companion.
  - Listen to what happens. Pick out one thought during the service that is new or challenging. Discuss these with friends or family after the service.
  - Volunteer to participate in worship services. You could offer a prayer, share a testimony, tell a story, minister through music, or prepare the worship space.

As worshipers we are invited to be active participants—to engage our minds, our emotions, our senses, and our energies as we seek God. Worship is the foundation of congregational life, and from these encounters with the Divine we are inspired to live as committed disciples of Jesus every day.

Fellowship Opportunities

One of the richest blessings in the world is the fellowship we enjoy with friends and family in the church. It is important, as a disciple of Jesus Christ, to cultivate friendships with other disciples. It is also important to help our congregation create opportunities through which we can introduce our friends to the fellowship of the church. With this in mind, we should take every opportunity to participate in the social life of our congregation. These events take many forms—potlucks, campfires, game nights, and the like. Whatever form they take, they are important opportunities for inviting friends and weaving our lives into the fabric of congregational relationships.

It is important for disciples to increase their understanding of the broader Christian tradition as well as other world religions. The spirit of ecumenical sharing with others gives a context for one's own faith and fosters peace through understanding.

Groups for Personal Growth

We do not grow alone. We need one another. With this in mind, many congregations offer small groups for our participation, ranging from Bible study groups to social groups. Two groups of particular interest are Covenant Discipleship Groups, which help us in our spiritual journey, and Witness Support Groups, which help us in sharing our witness with a friend. Sometimes congregations will have these and other groups operating, and we simply need to ask how and when we can join in. Other times these groups may not be active, and we may find that our inquiry about them is what "sparks" them into being. In any event, it is always appropriate to speak with our pastor about the group opportunities that are available.

Part of a Larger Church Community

One of the great blessings of life in the church is that we are members of a worldwide fellowship. Each congregation is a part of a group of congregations joined together in a common mission center. While mission centers exist to support local congregations, they also provide classes, family and youth camping experiences, workshops, and a variety of ministries that we can take advantage of. Likewise the Community of Christ offers special conference, worship, and educational opportunities sponsored by our World Church headquarters. Participating in mission center and World Church events helps broaden our horizons while giving us the opportunity to develop friendships with brothers and sisters in Christ from around our region and around the world.

We are members in a wonderful community—the Community of Christ. This community is here for us, and we, in return, enrich the community through our participation and sharing of our gifts. When we do, the affirmation lifted up in the Book of Mormon scripture can also be true of us: "…surely there could not be a happier people among all the people who had been created by the hand of God" (IV Nephi 1:19).

Chapter Seven:
Participating Faithfully

Scriptures for Reflection

They devoted themselves to the apostles' teaching and fellowship, to the breaking of bread and the prayers. Awe came upon everyone, because many wonders and signs were being done by the apostles. All who believed were together and had all things in common; they would sell their possessions and goods and distribute the proceeds to all, as any had need. Day by day, as they spent much time together in the temple, they broke bread at home and ate their food with glad and generous hearts, praising God and having the goodwill of all the people. And day by day the Lord added to their number those who were being saved.—Acts 2:42–47

And now, verily, verily I say unto thee, Put thy trust in that Spirit which leadeth to do good; yea, to do justly, to walk humbly, to judge righteously; and this is my Spirit. Verily, verily I say unto you, I will impart unto you of my Spirit, which shall enlighten your mind, which shall fill your soul with joy.—Doctrine and Covenants 10: 6–7a

In the New Testament, the book called the Acts of the Apostles describes the life of the disciples of Jesus in the earliest days. The book says that "they devoted themselves to the apostles' teaching and fellowship, to the breaking of bread and the prayers" (Acts 2:42). It goes on to say that they shared fully with each other, spent time together in worship, and enjoyed God's gifts to them in gladness.

To be a disciple of Jesus Christ is to be part of a community. We share our discipleship with each other. In doing so, we can strengthen and encourage each other.

The Heart of Discipleship

Discipleship in the Community of Christ begins with our mission statement: "We proclaim Jesus Christ and promote communities of joy, hope, love, and peace." Seeking ways to reflect this statement in your own life will lead you on a journey of spiritual growth and transformation. The following goals are for those taking the disciple's path:

- Share your witness and resources.
- Worship.
- Be involved.
- Learn.
- Be a peacemaker.

Share Your Witness and Resources

Becoming a disciple of Jesus Christ enriches our lives and creates a deep sense of satisfaction. People want to talk about this good news with others and share their resources so ministry can be brought to people worldwide.

- Invite others to share in congregational experiences. As we listen to others, we learn which activities and experiences might be of value in their lives.
- Share freely about what being a disciple of Jesus Christ has meant to you. We need not engage in deep doctrinal discussions; we can simply share what we have found in the gospel.
- Prioritize your spending in a way that provides for resources that can be given for the benefit of others. When we live in such a way, we honor our deepest values.
- Honor God's call to tithe. This is a generous, tangible response to God's grace and love, which helps meet the needs of an active church.

Worship

A disciple seeks to know God. The scriptures promise that God is always present and available to us. There are several things we can do to invite the Holy Spirit and realize God's presence in our lives.

- Engage in worship regularly with your congregation. Disciples help one another come to know God.
- Engage in personal worship and pray regularly. Disciples seek to be with God in times of quiet reflection.
- Seek inspiration and comfort from the scriptures. Reading the scriptures is a way to learn more about God and the guidelines for better living.

Be Involved

A disciple is a member of a community of disciples. By working and sharing together, we experience a deeper understanding of who God calls us to be.

- Embrace diversity. No two of us are alike, and we gain strength through our differences as well as through our similarities with others.
- Share in congregational activities. Through sharing together, we come to deeper understandings of our discipleship.
- Volunteer for specific tasks. We learn more about our discipleship as we attempt new things.

Learn

A disciple continually seeks to understand the life and ministry of Jesus. There is always more to know, and the church provides resources to guide you.

- Share in education experiences available in your congregation. Disciples seek to help one another in their learning.
- Study the scriptures. In addition to using the scriptures for personal worship, it is helpful to learn more about their background and meaning.
- Study widely in many subject areas. Knowledge of God can be found in many places, so reading books that are well written and researched can make us more effective disciples.

Be a Peacemaker

We are called to bring peace and justice to our world. In a world where people seek to dominate others, such a call is very much needed.

- Seek peace within yourself through spiritual disciplines, such as prayer. When we experience peace within ourselves, we are more able to share peace with others.
- Learn to use conflict-resolution skills and engage in ministries of reconciliation. Disciples learn how to bring peace to situations where conflict threatens to disrupt communities and relationships.
- Promote peace and seek justice. The world suffers when peace and justice are absent. Be an advocate.

Church Structure

Every congregation is part of a worldwide church fellowship. This means that congregations support each other. Congregations are joined together in jurisdictions called mission centers. Mission centers offer training opportunities and special programs. They also provide administrative support to congregational officers.

Mission centers help small congregations have access to resources and programs similar to those available to very large congregations. A mission center is led by a mission center president and a mission center financial officer. It is governed by a mission center conference. The conference may be composed of all members of a mission center or by delegates elected by each congregation. Sharing in mission center conferences and other activities will help you to be more familiar with the ministries the church provides.

Mission centers receive administrative and ministerial guidance from a field apostle. There are twelve apostles, who are called to provide special ministry and leadership to the church throughout the world.

The First Presidency (the president of the church and two counselors) provide leadership and ministry to the entire church. They are especially called to help the church understand the gospel and the mission of the church.

The Presiding Bishopric (the church's presiding bishop and two counselors) helps the church to understand the relationship between its ministry and the tangible resources we have been given as individuals and as a church.

How Will You Be Involved?

The ministry of every member is important. It is essential that every disciple seek to understand God's call for ministry and mutual support. In the church, every one of us can find opportunities to serve God and each other. Talk with your pastor about ways you can serve in joy and gratitude.

Chapter Eight:
Generosity—Sharing Our Witness

Scriptures for Reflection

> *I appeal to you therefore, brothers and sisters, by the mercies of God, to present your bodies as a living sacrifice, holy and acceptable to God, which is your spiritual worship. Do not be conformed to this world, but be transformed by the renewing of your minds, so that you may discern what is the will of God—what is good and acceptable and perfect.*
>
> —Romans 12:1–2

> *Let my word be preached to the bruised and the brokenhearted as well as those who are enmeshed in sin, longing to repent and follow me. Let the truths of my gospel be proclaimed as widely and as far as the dedication of the Saints, especially through the exercise of their temporal stewardship, will allow. My Spirit is reaching out to numerous souls even now and there are many who will respond if you, my people, will bear affirmative testimony of my love and my desires for all to come unto me.*—Doctrine and Covenants 153:9a–b

As disciples of Jesus Christ, we accept responsibility for sharing generously with others. Our sharing is in response to the gift of God's love for every person. We share our witness of Jesus Christ and our resources. Sharing with others acknowledges that all we have and are is a gift from God to us. Sharing our witness tells others what Jesus Christ and the church mean to us.

Shaping Our Witness

When Jesus called his first disciples, he simply invited them to follow him. He invited them to develop a relationship with him. Jesus promised that he would use them to invite others into a new life. "Follow me, and I will make you fish for people" (Matthew 4:19). Discipleship is about our responding to Jesus' invitation and helping others find new life in him. Our witness is shaped by the following considerations:

- Our relationship with Jesus Christ brings new meaning, purpose, and hope, which is summed up in the word "salvation."
- Our relationship with the Community of Christ brings a sense of acceptance, belonging, and mission.
- Other people are searching for what we have found.
- Listening, identifying needs, and sharing our witness makes a difference.
- God is actively involved in the process of making disciples.

"My Spirit is reaching out to numerous souls even now and there are many who will respond if you, my people, will bear affirmative testimony of my love and my desires for all to come unto me" (Doctrine and Covenants 153:9b). Being a disciple is about claiming this promise. As we share in the witness of God's love and divine invitation, many will respond.

Identifying Your Personal Testimony

We believe that each disciple has a testimony of Christ's love to share. It is a gift from God. It is unique and special. Your story can focus on a specific event, time, and place. It may be a series of experiences over time that led to a growing understanding of God, Christ, the Holy Spirit, and yourself. The key is to identify your testimony. The following questions may be helpful:

- What was my life like before developing a relationship with Jesus Christ?
- What changes have I made as a result of this relationship?
- What was missing in my life? How has that emptiness been filled?
- What difference does participating in the Community of Christ make?
- How have prayer, scripture study, and experiencing the sacraments affected me?

As you respond to these questions, your personal testimony emerges. The next step is developing confidence to share your testimony with others.

Overcoming the Barriers

Witnessing is easier for some disciples than for others. It is natural to have reservations. Uncertainty about what to share, with whom, and when are common concerns, even for those who have a strong desire to witness. Acknowledging that barriers exist is a positive step. Some of the most common reasons for not witnessing are listed below, along with a suggested response.

- *Talking about religion might offend.* Develop a caring relationship first; then, frame your testimony with the other person's need in mind.
- *Difficult questions might be asked.* Not knowing all the answers is positive. It gives opportunity to find an answer and share again later.
- *Witnessing takes a lot of time.* Discipleship is about new priorities, including real care and concern for another person.
- *Others can do it better.* Maybe so, but you are called to give a unique witness of your own experience. Only you can do it.

Whatever the barrier might be, there are resources available to give support.

- Prayer is the disciple's most important resource. Asking the Holy Spirit for courage to share your witness makes a difference.
- Mutual support from other witnesses strengthens us as disciples. We can form a witness support group in our congregation, which provides us with a small-group support system of others who are sharing their testimonies too.
- Missionary resources are available for personal witnessing training and for giving to those who ask about the church. (For more information contact the Missionary Ministries Office, 1001 W. Walnut, Independence, MO 64050; 1-800-825-2806, ext. 2242.)

Invite! Invite! Invite!

The scriptures contain many stories of new disciples telling their family and friends about Jesus and inviting them to come and meet him (John 1:40–45). Newly baptized disciples often have friends and family who may also be open to "meeting" Jesus. They simply need to be invited. The witness of invitation can happen in various ways.

- Invite someone to have a conversation.
- Invite someone to share a meal.
- Invite someone to help.
- Invite someone to a congregational activity planned for guests.
- Invite someone to read a missionary tract.
- Invite someone to share in a recreational activity.
- Invite someone to make a commitment.

Disciples of Jesus Christ accept the responsibility to invite others. We do it many times each week, especially with our friends, neighbors, and family. It is what we do. Our challenge is to see each opportunity for invitation as an opportunity for witness. Our goal is to offer the invitation and to witness of what we do and who we are as disciples of Jesus Christ. One strategy can be to make a written list of people we know who might possibly be open to our invitation and witness. We then list upcoming invitational opportunities we think might be appropriate for them. We pray and expect in faith that we will be led to share wisely the good news we have found in Christ and the church.

The Congregation as a Witnessing Community

Disciples are also responsible for helping their congregation be a witnessing community. Such a community is Christ centered and people oriented. It is intentional about creating ministries that invite, welcome, accept, baptize, and disciple those who come. In support of this congregational mission, the disciple

- invites friends to share in congregational ministries;
- assists in planning "come and see" activities designed for guests;
- helps create an atmosphere of hospitality and personally greets each new person;
- actively encourages missionary-focused ministries to include witness support groups, inquirer's classes, prebaptismal classes for all ages, guest-friendly worship, and home missionary ministry sessions; and
- serves as a mentor to newly baptized disciples.

Guiding Others to Discipleship

> Behold, I am a disciple of Jesus Christ, the Son of God. I have been called of him to declare his word among his people, that they might have everlasting life.—III Nephi 2:97

Guiding others into a relationship with Jesus Christ is our mission and joy. Our discipleship calls us to take the following steps:

1. Seek constantly to follow the example of Jesus Christ in all things.
2. Identify our personal testimony for the purpose of sharing with others.
3. Develop our courage and confidence to witness, especially when it is not always easy to do so.
4. Invite others into a relationship of mutual sharing.
5. Help our congregation become Christ centered and people oriented.

Being a disciple is about inviting all to be disciples. Mature disciples mentor new disciples of Jesus Christ as a sacred responsibility. We commit our resources to the faith development of other disciples. We are with them as they form their witness. We support them through prayer, example, and friendship. Together we live with them the disciple's generous response.

Chapter Nine:
Generosity—Sharing Our Resources

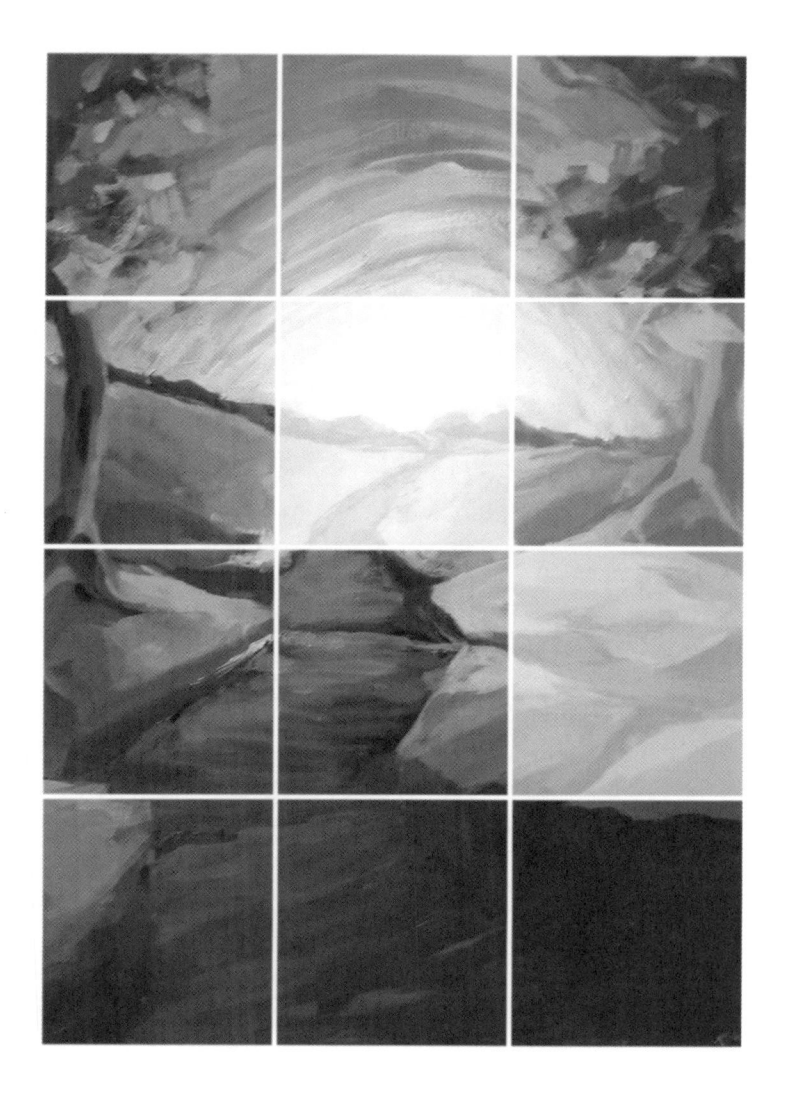

Scriptures for Reflection

I appeal to you therefore, brothers and sisters, by the mercies of God, to present your bodies as a living sacrifice, holy and acceptable to God, which is your spiritual worship. Do not be conformed to this world, but be transformed by the renewing of your minds, so that you may discern what is the will of God—what is good and acceptable and perfect.

—Romans 12:1–2

Let my word be preached to the bruised and the brokenhearted as well as those who are enmeshed in sin, longing to repent and follow me. Let the truths of my gospel be proclaimed as widely and as far as the dedication of the Saints, especially through the exercise of their temporal stewardship, will allow. My Spirit is reaching out to numerous souls even now and there are many who will respond if you, my people, will bear affirmative testimony of my love and my desires for all to come unto me.

—Doctrine and Covenants 153:9a–b

As disciples of Jesus Christ, we accept responsibility for sharing generously with others. Our sharing is in response to the gift of God's love for every person. We share our witness of Jesus Christ and our resources. Sharing with others acknowledges that all we have and are is a gift from God to us. Sharing our witness tells others what Jesus Christ and the church mean to us.

Sharing Our Resources: A Disciple's Generous Response

Receiving First

Part of our witness as disciples is sharing the news of God's great generosity. God provides "enough and to spare" (Doctrine and Covenants 101:2f). God shares in abundance, "good measure, pressed down…shaken together, and running over." All that we have and all that we are is a priceless gift to us from God. What then is our response as disciples of Jesus Christ? In simple terms, we respond with thankfulness and share with others as generously as God has shared with us.

Scripture guides us in our discipleship: "Stewardship is the response of my people to the ministry of my Son and is required alike of all those who seek to build the kingdom" (Doctrine and Covenants 147:5a). All things were created by God and are to be used for God's purposes. As disciples of Christ, we explore the scriptures to understand our stewardship of time, giftedness, and resources in response to God's grace and love expressed to us in the life of Jesus Christ. Our stewardship is

- a personal response to God's grace and love;
- a means to meet the needs of a growing church; and
- a way to provide more fully and joyfully for Christlike service and ministry, locally and globally.

Agency is one of the generous gifts God gives to us. Agency is our ability to choose freely how we respond to God's infinite love and grace. Using our agency wisely allows us to manage our time, giftedness, and resources to benefit our personal, family, congregational, and community life. More specifically, our stewardship of financial resources defines the extent we can generously share, wisely save, and responsibly spend. The following principles of A Disciple's Generous Response guide us in living out our stewardship of resources:

- Disciples practice generosity as a spiritual discipline in response to God's grace and love.
- Disciples are faithful in response to Christ's ministry.
- A disciple's financial response, while unique to individual circumstances, expresses love of God, neighbor, creation, and self.

- Disciples share generously through tithing so that others may experience God's generosity.
- Disciples save wisely in order to create a better tomorrow for themselves, their family, the mission of the church, and the world.
- Disciples spend responsibly as a commitment to live in health and harmony with God and the world.

Share through Tithing

Tithing is a concept deeply rooted in our scriptures. It is our gift to God in response to God's generous gifts of grace and love to us. Generosity comes from a spirit of thankfulness within us, not from imposed formulas and rules. We share what we have because we want to. We share what we receive first from God. Therefore, a disciple asks, "How much tithing can I hope to share?" rather than, "How much should I give?"

Tithing is based on the biblical principle of sharing our firstfruits with God. This means tithing is the disciple's response of thanksgiving and is given before we spend or save from our income. In the Bible the word "tithe" means a tenth part of what one owns or receives. Tithing, according to scriptural principles, is the act of sharing 10 percent of our income with God. As disciples we honor what we have received from God by reaching toward sharing 10 percent or more through Mission and Community Tithes. "Let whoever is of a generous heart bring the Lord's offering" (Exodus 35:5).

Our Mission Tithes go primarily to World and Congregation Ministries. Through them we support world and local missions that fulfill the following scripture: "Let the truths of my gospel be proclaimed as widely and as far as the dedication of the Saints, especially through the exercise of their temporal stewardship will allow" (Doctrine and Covenants 153:9a). Mission Tithes are a significant portion of a generous disciple's response. By sharing equally with Congregation and World Ministries, the disciple shares in the mission of the church both on a local and global level. Examples of Mission Tithes include Congregation Ministries, Mission Center Ministries, World Ministries, Oblation, World Hunger, and other designated church funds.

Disciples generally give Mission Tithes during worship services. In your home congregation, you can request offering envelopes from your congregation's financial officer. Offering envelopes allow you to designate funds for World Ministries and Congregation Ministries, or give to other funds such as the Building Fund or Oblation Fund. Additionally some disciples share through direct contributions sent to world headquarters. Estate and financial planning ministers at world headquarters are also available, on request, to provide assistance in planning other ways for you to share Mission and Community Tithes.

Community Tithes are a disciple's response to church-affiliated organizations and other charitable nonprofit organizations that are "in the forefront...recognizing the worth of persons and committed to bringing the ministry of my Son to bear on their lives" (Doctrine and Covenants 151:9). Generous disciples may share a portion of their tithing directly with institutions such as Graceland University, Outreach International, Outreach Europe, Restoration Trail Foundation, SaintsCare, World Accord, and other charitable nonprofit organizations.

Save for the Future

The principle of saving is an expression of hope for the future. Disciples save in order to create a better tomorrow for themselves, their heirs, the church, and the world. Through planning and careful management, many have found that saving at least 10 percent of their income is an effective way to prepare for the future. "For which of you, intending to build a tower, does not sit down and estimate the cost, to see whether he has enough to complete it?" (Luke 14:28). Disciples save for a number of reasons: major purchases, unexpected needs, vacations, retirement funds, college funds, and estate building for family and church. Indeed, disciples can continue their generous response beyond this life by making provisions in their estates for the ongoing ministries of the church.

Spend Responsibly

The principle of spending responsibly is a commitment by disciples to use the remainder of their income to live in health and harmony as they support family, personal needs, giftedness, and interests. Wise and prayerful planning and management of these remaining resources brings financial wholeness in life. How we spend our money is part of our personal witness of Christ. "It is incumbent upon the Saints…to be in the world but not of it, living and acting honestly and honorably before God and in the sight of all men, using the things of this world in the manner designed of God, that the places where they occupy may shine as Zion…" (Doctrine and Covenants 128:8b,c). Disciples spend responsibly in all areas of life, including housing, health care, transportation, food, clothing, recreation, and personal development.

Live as a Generous Disciple

Generosity is one of the ways we can both honor our heritage and our call to live as prophetic people who help shape the future God has envisioned for all creation. A Disciple's Generous Response is a whole life commitment we choose to make in response to God's wonderful generosity. We express our gratitude to God with each breath of life we take as we share generously, save wisely, and spend responsibly. Understanding our stewardship at the personal, congregational, and denominational levels will bless us spiritually and grow us as a community, so that we can respond "more fully and joyfully for the great work to which [we] are called" and engaged (Doctrine and Covenants 154:5b).

For additional information and recommended resources, please visit the Presiding Bishopric home page at *http://www.CofChrist.org/bishop*.

Chapter Ten:
Serving in the Mission of Christ

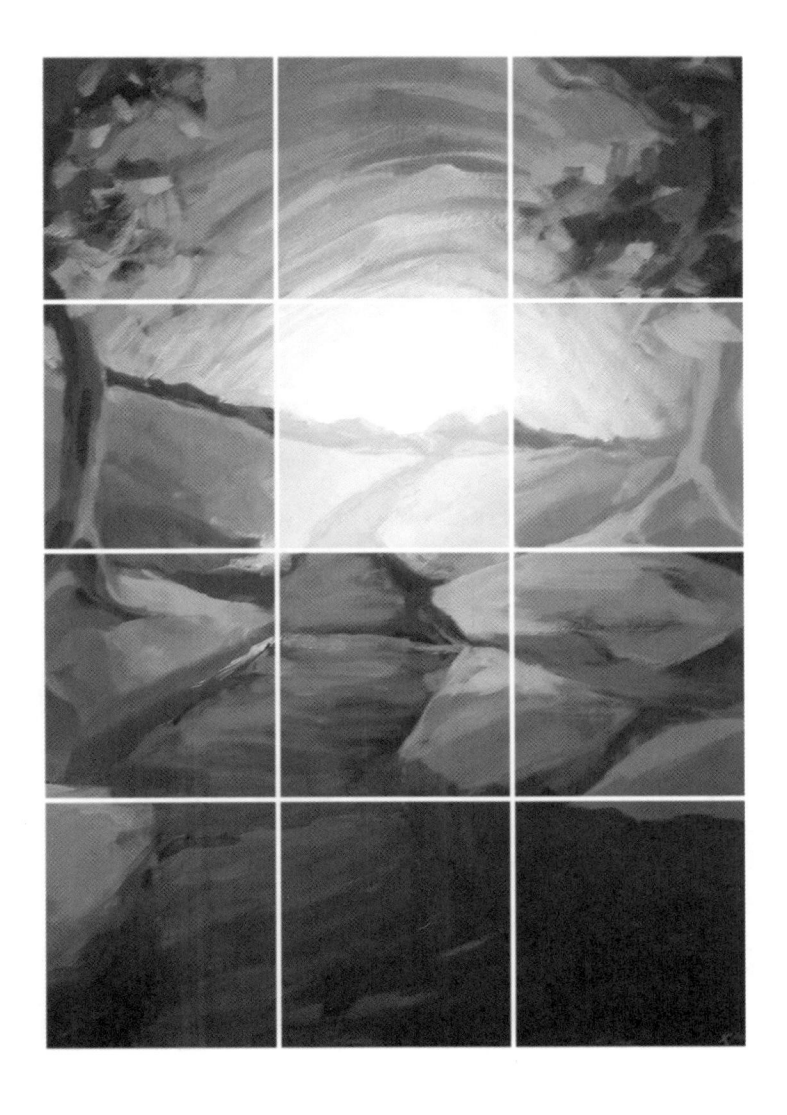

Scriptures for Reflection

And Jesus came and said to them, "All authority in heaven and on earth has been given to me. Go therefore and make disciples of all nations, baptizing them in the name of the Father and of the Son and of the Holy Spirit, and teaching them to obey everything that I have commanded you. And remember, I am with you always, to the end of the age."
—Matthew 28:18–20

Blessed are they who shall seek to bring forth my Zion at that day, for they shall have the gift and the power of the Holy Ghost...—I Nephi 3:187

The Mission of Christ

Jesus began his ministry with these words: "The time is fulfilled, and the kingdom of God has come near; repent and believe in the good news" (Mark 1:14). The Gospel of Mark gives the headlines. Jesus proclaims the coming kingdom of God. We are invited to change, repent, and believe this very good news.

But what does Jesus mean by the kingdom? Luke's account of the beginning of Jesus' ministry helps us. Jesus reads this scripture from Isaiah 61:1–2 and 58:6 in his home synagogue in Nazareth:

> The Spirit of the Lord is upon me,
> because he has anointed me
> to bring good news to the poor.
> He has sent me to proclaim release to the captives
> and recovery of sight to the blind,
> to let the oppressed go free,
> to proclaim the year of the Lord's favor.—Luke 4:18–19

The kingdom is good news to the poor, those in prison, those who are handicapped, and those who are oppressed and exploited. In this kingdom task Jesus knows the power of the Holy Spirit upon him. As we read in the Gospels, we see how Jesus invites others to follow him, become his disciples, and learn from him. This same Holy Spirit is promised us in the same tasks of being good news to the poor and all who are vulnerable.

The good news of Jesus Christ is the story of Pentecost told by Luke in the Acts of the Apostles, chapter two. The chapter begins by the disciples receiving the Holy Spirit. Peter then proclaims Jesus Christ and invites the crowd to be baptized. The chapter ends with the disciples sharing all that they had with one another. In the early Jerusalem church two thousand years ago, we have an example set for us in which Jesus is being proclaimed and a Spirit-filled community is being created that is good news to the poor. This kind of community we call Zion:

> And the Lord called his people Zion, because they were of one heart and one mind, and dwelt in righteousness; and there was no poor among them....—Doctrine and Covenants 36:2h–i

As we seek to bring about Zion, we are promised the power of the Holy Spirit. Today the mission of the Community of Christ is the same as the mission of the early church: We proclaim Jesus Christ and promote communities of joy, hope, love, and peace.

We proclaim Jesus Christ…

A living relationship with Jesus Christ is the path to fullness of life. That is why we call Jesus savior: he brings salvation, which is the restoration of wholeness. We proclaim Jesus in two ways:

1. By how we live.

We proclaim Jesus by how we live and by the love we show. Together as a community, we are the body of Christ in the world (I Corinthians 12:1–31). Inspired and energized by the Holy Spirit, we show what Jesus is like. As we feed the hungry, visit those in prison, care for the sick, and welcome the stranger, we are Jesus to them and they to us, as people with mutual vulnerabilities (Matthew 25:31–46).

As individuals we also proclaim Christ by our personal honesty, our faithfulness to Christ, in the kinds of jobs we choose, and in how we use our time, talents, and money. Our commitment to be reconciled—to be faithful in our marriages, to tell the truth, and to love our enemies—proclaims Christ to those around us (Matthew 5:21–48). When we fail, we confess it and show that repentance and change is a life-long process in us. When we are transparent about our struggles and reliance on the grace of God to forgive and transform us, we give hope to other struggling people.

2. By what we say.

The way we live will provoke questions. People will want to know what makes us different. We can be ready for these times with gentleness and kindness, in order to give the reasons for the hope that is within us (I Peter 3:15–16). We can be ready with our story of how Christ has blessed us. We can be ready to invite others as friends to our church fellowship. When Jesus commanded us to make disciples of all nations, he meant all people of all races, ethnic backgrounds, and nationalities. All are invited. All are called. We are called to witness of Jesus Christ and the equal worth of all people.

We promote communities of joy, hope, love, and peace.

Together we seek to model a community we call Zion, the kingdom of God on earth. We want to be a changed community that will inspire the world with hope and new possibilities. We begin in our congregations. Our commitment to the local fellowship is very important, but we are also part of a larger international church present in more than fifty nations. Our community is local and global. Our commitment is local and global.

An excellent test of Christian community is to ask, "How are the children, and how are the elderly?" Any community that is good for the young and old, both of whom are vulnerable, is more likely to be good for everyone. These questions can also be applied to our neighborhoods, villages, towns, cities, and nations. Specifically, "How are the children?" If anything is good for children, we can support and praise it. If anything damages or hurts or threatens children, then we work for change.

"Do we hand a better world on to our children and grandchildren?" is an important question to keep asking. It raises important questions about the environment, and about peace and justice for everyone in the world. By using the welfare of all children as the measuring stick for the health of community, we can ask critical and searching questions of ourselves, our neighborhoods, our schools and governments. At the same time we can work together united in our concern for children. We are inspired by how Jesus loved children and taught that they were the center of the kingdom (Mark 9:33–37, 42–48; 10:1–16). A world good for all children and for future generations is Zion fully come. Indeed, it is good for all generations.

The church seal reminds us that a little child shall lead us in the ways of peace (see Isaiah 11:6).

Community of Christ

We live in a hurting world. Yet we believe that it was created by a loving God who longs for it to be healed. Following Jesus Christ and inspired by the Holy Spirit, we can make a positive, significant difference in the world. We are needed in the task of pursuing peace, reconciliation, and healing of the spirit. We work though our local congregation and join in mutual purpose with our sisters and brothers all over the world who are seeking to live out their Christian discipleship. We affirm that serving in the mission of Christ is a great and marvelous work to which we all can give ourselves. We give God praise for our opportunity and privilege to serve in the cause of Zion.

Chapter Eleven:
Basic Beliefs of the
Community of Christ

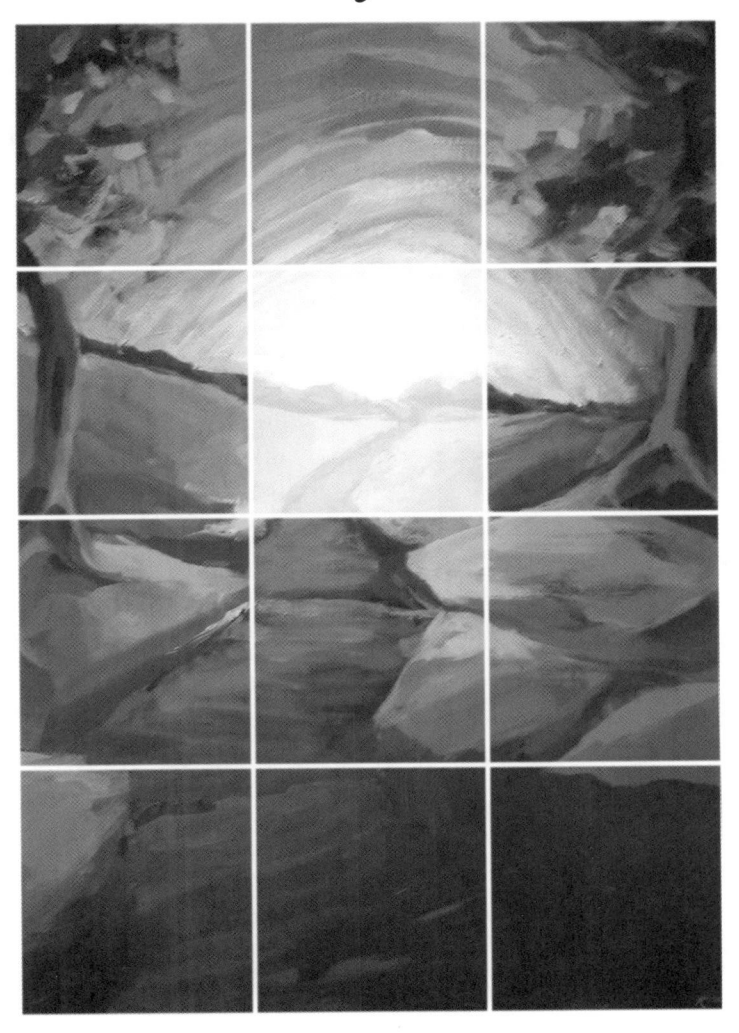

Scriptures for Reflection

Hold to the standard of sound teaching that you have heard from me, in the faith and love that are in Christ Jesus. Guard the good treasure entrusted to you, with the help of the Holy Spirit living in us.—II Timothy 1:13–14

Claim your unique and sacred place within the circle of those who call upon the name of Jesus Christ. Be faithful to the spirit of the Restoration, mindful that it is a spirit of adventure, openness, and searching.
—Doctrine and Covenants 161:1b

Our Faith and Beliefs

We recognize that the perception of truth is always qualified by human nature and experience. Consequently there is no official church creed that must be accepted by all members. Through the years, however, various statements, such as those below, have been developed to present generally accepted beliefs within the church. We are encouraged to study the scriptures, to participate in the life and mission of the church, and to examine our own experiences as we grow in understanding and response to the gospel of Jesus Christ. Each beginning paragraph is an official statement of faith and beliefs in the Community of Christ and can be found in the Community of Christ tract "Faith and Beliefs."

God

The one eternal, living God is triune: one God in three persons. The God who meets us in the testimony of Israel is the same God who meets us in Jesus Christ, and who indwells creation as the Holy Spirit. God is the Eternal Creator, the source of love, life, and truth. God actively loves and cares for each person. All things that exist owe their being to God. God alone is worthy of our worship.

Our faith statements about God grow out of our deepest experiences of life. The Community of Christ does not base its convictions about God on clever arguments. Rather, it trusts and it believes. To believe in God is to be committed to God and God's will for us and all creation. To believe in God is to give ourselves in trust to the purposes of God, who continues to seek us always.

Jesus Christ

> Jesus Christ is "God with us," the Son of God, and the living expression of God in the flesh. Jesus Christ lived, was crucified, died, and rose again. The nature, love, and purpose of God are most clearly seen in Jesus Christ, our Savior.

Christian faith is historical. It does not grow out of philosophy or any general principles of religion. Christian faith comes from the revelation of the living God in and through the events of history. Jesus, professed by the church as the Christ, reveals God to us. He is fully human and fully divine. The nature of God is most clearly revealed through him. Jesus the Christ is the point of reference that illuminates our entire faith. As Christians, we look to Jesus' words and deeds, to his death on the cross for us, and to his risen presence among us.

Spirit

> The Holy Spirit is the continuing presence of God in the world. The Spirit works in our minds and hearts through intelligence, comfort, guidance, love, and power to sustain, inspire, and remake us.

God is "with us" and "for us," as revealed in Jesus Christ. God is also at work "in us" through the continuing presence of the Holy Spirit. The Holy Spirit works within our community of faith to conform us to the image of Jesus, God's Son. Within the church, gifts of worship and ministry express the work of the Holy Spirit. The Holy Spirit empowers disciples to witness to others by helping them develop their gifts of faith.

Salvation

God loves us even though we are sinful. Through the ministry of Christ and the presence of the Holy Spirit, we are able to turn to God and to receive the gifts of salvation and eternal life. Those who accept the gospel are called to respond to Christ through baptism and committed discipleship. As individuals exercise faith in Christ and follow his example and teachings, they become new people.

Salvation comes from God through the person and redemptive work of Jesus Christ. God's love revealed in Jesus Christ confronts human evil to save us from our sin. God's grace does not leave us alone, even in our separation from God. Remarkably, through grace, God's love so embraces us that, by the power of the Holy Spirit and our faith, we experience our lives transformed into new life in Christ. By God's grace we are turned from rebellion, healed from sin, renewed by the Holy Spirit, and called to discipleship.

The Church

Christian discipleship is most fully possible when it is pursued in a community of committed believers. The church, as part of the body of Christ, is the means through which the ministry of Christ continues in the world today. It is a community of people seeking to bring God's love to all through compassionate ministry, worship, the sacraments, and witness.

As part of the universal Christian family, the Community of Christ continues to seek to understand its unique call. We want to express our Christian discipleship faithfully. We follow Jesus Christ willingly and enthusiastically. As his followers, we answer our call to be centered in God's love in Jesus Christ. The Holy Spirit empowers us to service and witness. The scriptures warn us not to be self-serving. We remember we are called to *re*-present

God's redemptive and reconciling actions in the world. Our church seeks to make real and visible the loving community that belongs to God's very nature as Father, Son, and Holy Spirit.

Revelation

> The process through which God reveals divine will and love is called revelation. God continues to reveal today as in the past. God is revealed to us through scripture, the faith community, prayer, nature, and in human history.

Revelation is God's gracious act of making known divine identity and purpose. In a free act of love and will, God makes God's self available to be known. In this, God does not cease to be a mystery. Revelation discloses God through particular circumstances, events, and people. Understanding revelation requires our personal response and appropriation as an interpretive focus of its content and meaning.

Revelation is always a disturbing event. It may even be shocking and disruptive. It surprises us with new, unexpected glimpses of God acting in the world. Revelation calls us into faithful, loving relationship with God and all that God creates.

Scripture

> The scriptures provide divine guidance and inspired insight for life when responsibly interpreted and faithfully applied. With other Christians, we affirm the Bible as scripture for the church. In our tradition, the Book of Mormon and the Doctrine and Covenants are additional scriptural witnesses of God's love and Christ's ministry.

Scripture is the unique and irreplaceable witness to the saving and transforming message of the gospel of Jesus Christ with which God has entrusted the church. The church formed the canon of scripture so that it might always have a way to hear the good news. Scripture nurtures our faith, measures our life, tests our experience, and helps us remember our identity. Scripture reveals God in and through the humanity of its writers, not separate from them. Scripture's authority resides in the example of Christ, who came to be servant (Mark 10:45). Therefore scripture serves to witness that Jesus is Christ. Using it to oppress, control, or dominate others is contrary to the saving purposes of God. If Jesus came to serve and not be served, then how much more should books that point to him be treated as a servant—records to the saving purposes of God? When we, the church, faithfully attend to scripture, God's word lives and continues to be revealed anew in us.

Sacraments

> The sacraments express the continuing presence of Christ through the church. They help us establish and continually renew our relationship with God. Through them we establish or reaffirm our covenant with God in response to God's grace. The sacraments of the church are: baptism, confirmation of membership, the Lord's Supper (Communion), marriage, blessing of children, administration to the sick, ordination to the priesthood, and the evangelist's blessing.

Sacraments are physical expressions of God's grace celebrated within the church. They are testimonies of the love of God in Jesus Christ that we experience through the presence of the Holy Spirit in our community of faith. Sacraments help disciples remember and reenact significant elements of the gospel. Through the sacraments, the Holy Spirit communicates grace, and we receive forgiveness, renewal, and the blessing of God's love. The sacraments energize and refresh our experience of Jesus Christ, in whom is our faith, hope, love, and peace.

Human Worth

> God loves each of us equally and unconditionally. All people have great worth and should be respected as creations of God with basic human rights. The willingness to love and accept others is essential to faithfulness to the gospel of Christ.

As the Community of Christ we affirm that people are of great worth (Doctrine and Covenants 16:3c) and are created that they might have joy (II Nephi 1:115). Humanity is endowed with freedom and created to know, love, and serve God. We are created in the image of God and find our true worth and identity in relating to God and each other. We are restless. We yearn for responsible, Christ-like relationships. We express our worth through the life of a disciple, disciplined by faith, hope, love, and peace.

All Are Called

All men, women, youth, and children are given gifts and abilities to enhance life and to become involved in Christ's mission. Some are called to particular responsibility as ordained ministers (priesthood) in the church. The church provides for a wide range of priesthood ministries through calling and ordination of men and women.

All are called according to the gifts of God. The primary call of every person is to be a disciple of Jesus Christ and follow the example that he set. Each person has particular gifts that determine and enable calling and service. Through the discernment of the Holy Spirit, presiding officers with authority in the church are prompted through wisdom and revelation to call and ordain people to specific priesthood ministries. Priesthood ministries serve individuals, families, and the larger community by offering the witness of preaching, teaching, pastoral care, celebration of sacraments, ministry of presence, and directing the affairs of the church.

Free Agency

All people are free to choose, resulting in real consequences of good and evil to our lives, the lives of others, and our environment. Commitment to Christ, sensitivity to the Holy Spirit, and participation in the faith community help us to make responsible choices that enhance human life and respect creation.

As a community of faith we affirm that we belong to God and to each other. The quality of our relationships depends on the exercise of our freedom and ability to choose wisely. Freedom is a gift God imparted to us at our creation. We are free to be responsible. We have liberty, and God holds us accountable for how we use it. God asks each of us how we have exercised the freedom of our opportunities in all aspects of life.

Stewardship

> All things were created by God and should be used for God's purposes. Stewardship is the wise management of gifts and resources to enrich personal, family, congregational, and community life, as well as natural resources for the good of all creation.

God creates, loves, and blesses us. Stewardship is our response to God's grace and love. Disciples of Jesus Christ are stewards. We are stewards of all that we have. Everything we have comes ultimately from God, for "the earth is the Lord's" (Psalm 24:1). We are stewards of the gospel, the good news that comes to us in Jesus Christ. We are stewards of the earth also. We are accountable to God for everything entrusted to us. It is for our use, for other's benefit, and for the gospel witness.

The Kingdom

> God's kingdom is present wherever people acknowledge the lordship of God over life, relationships, and creation. The full coming of the kingdom awaits the final victory over evil when divine rule is established and justice, peace, and righteousness prevail.

In the midst of a faithless, self-serving world, the church proclaims the kingdom of God both as a present reality and as a future hope. The church acknowledges the total sovereignty of God over all human life and endeavor. Christian faith is an expectant faith, rooted in God's freedom and love. It eagerly awaits completion of God's creative and redemptive activity. The prospect of the kingdom of God on earth calls the Community of Christ to pursue peace, reconciliation, and healing of the spirit (Doctrine and Covenants 156:5a) for today's world.

Zion

> The "cause of Zion" expresses our commitment to pursuing God's kingdom through the establishment of Christ-centered communities in families, congregations, neighborhoods, cities, and throughout the world.

Members of the Community of Christ are summoned by the "cause of Zion." We hope that the community-forming love of God will be expressed in human communities as disciples witness to God's grace extended to all creation. Our prophetic church participates in the world to embody Zion as God's divine intent for all personal and social relationships. Zion implements the concrete principles, processes, and relationships of the gospel of Jesus Christ that realize the kingdom of God in the world.

Peace

> Because of our commitment to Christ and belief in the worth of all people and the value of community building, we dedicate our lives to the pursuit of peace and justice for all people.

We affirm that the gospel of Jesus Christ impacts the common structures of human existence with God's reconciling and redeeming love. Jesus is our peace (Ephesians 2:14). As disciples of Jesus we are called to practice disciplines of peace. We combine our influence for peace through the church community. Jesus Christ, the Prince of Peace, summons us to proclaim and pursue peace and justice for all in the world.

Resurrection

God conserves and renews life as revealed in the resurrection of Jesus Christ, a sign of God's ultimate victory over death. In Christ's resurrection, we find hope and courage for living. Through resurrection, God transforms individuals, bringing them into the fullness of eternal life.

The hope of the church is centered always on the glory of God. The resurrection of the crucified Jesus reveals God's glory and our future. Christ's resurrection is a revelation of God's promise of new life for all humanity and all creation. It is in the hope of resurrection that Christians find courage to live in a world full of distortion, deception, corruption, and death. God's purpose in history culminates in the incalculable gift disclosed in Jesus' resurrection from the dead. Because of Jesus' resurrection, death is not the last word about our lives. We have hope for eternal life—life freed forever from the power of death.

Judgment

Our eternal destiny is determined by God according to divine wisdom and love and according to our response to God's call to us. God's judgment is just and is based on the kind of people we have become in relation to the potential of our lives.

Judgment reminds us we are not our own. We are created by God in God's image. We are accountable for the gift of life. All creation, including humanity, has been formed to respond to the ends for which it was created. All forms of life will share in God's judgment. Together they will acknowledge the Creator who fashioned them.

End Time

God is acting in history to reconcile all of creation to divine purpose. The meaning and end to which history moves is revealed in Jesus Christ. The ultimate victory of righteousness and peace over injustice, evil, and sin is assured because of the unfailing love of God and the conviction that Christ is coming again.

The Community of Christ believes that the inner meaning and end toward which all history moves is revealed in Jesus Christ, our Lord. Jesus' resurrection and victory over the grave attests to our conviction that Christ will come again. The promise of his coming kindles our hope and inspires our confidence that God's purpose for the whole creation will be fulfilled.

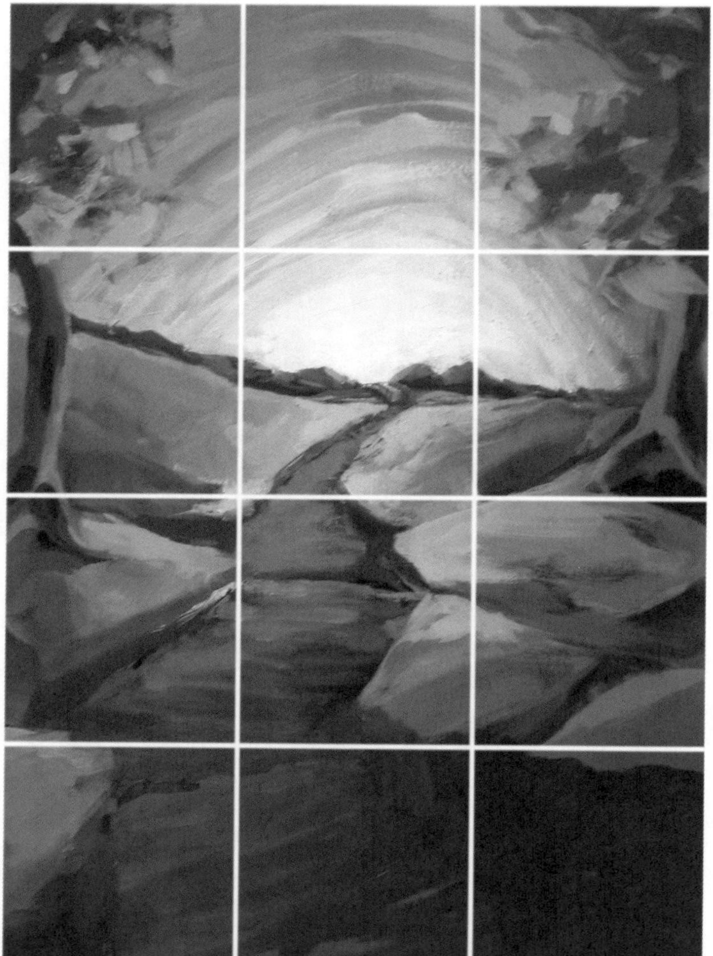

Resources

Community of Christ denominational Web site:
www.CofChrist.org

Face to Face, a quarterly spirituality journal:
www.CofChrist.org/facetoface

Herald House Catalog and Web site, containing a complete listing of Community of Christ denominational resources and literature: *www.HeraldHouse.org*

Herald, the monthly denominational magazine:
www.CofChrist.org/Herald

Presiding Bishopric home page:
www.CofChrist.org/bishop